Help
at Home

by Emma Buckley

 HOUGHTON MIFFLIN HARCOURT
School Publishers

PHOTOGRAPHY CREDITS: Cover © Michael Newman/PhotoEdit; 1 © Alamy; 2 © Getty Images/Digital Vision; 3 © Kayte M. Deioma/PhotoEdit; 4 © Alamy; 5 © Geri Engberg/The Image Works; 6 © Alamy; 7 © Jonathan Nourok/PhotoEdit; 8 © Alamy; 9 © Alamy; 10 © Michael Newman/PhotoEdit

Printed in China

ISBN-13: 978-0-547-42744-7
ISBN-10: 0-547-42744-1

2 3 4 5 6 7 8 0940 18 17 16 15 14 13 12 11 10

Families work at home.
There are many **different** jobs to do.
The work can get done fast if we all help.

Sam always makes his bed.
But he can't reach the bed
on the top.
It's too high!

Dad washes the clothes.
When they are dry,
Jen helps fold them.
She is happy to help.

Katie plays with toys.
She reads stories, too.
Once she is done, she
puts her things away.

June helps set the table.
She puts out the plates.
Then she puts forks and
spoons <mark>near</mark> the plates.

If some food falls
on the floor, Pam helps
clean up the mess.

Grandpa wants to plant
flowers in the yard.
Rob helps him dig and
plant to make a garden.

The boys help Dad
give Sandy a bath.
They must use enough
water to wash her.

There are lots of jobs to
do at home.
What can you do to help
your family at home?

Responding

WORDS TO KNOW **Word Builder**

What word do you know that means the opposite of <mark>different</mark>?

Write About It

Text to Self Draw a picture of something you do to help at your house. Write a sentence to tell about your picture. Use a vocabulary word in your answer.

always	**high**
different	**near**
enough	**once**
happy	**stories**

✔ **TARGET STRATEGY** **Analyze/Evaluate**

Tell how you feel about the text, and why.